Some night's th

others they'

but I still can't seen

Some nights they're silent,

others they're loud,

but I still can't seem to drown them out.

Some nights they're mean,

others they're playful,

but I still can't seem excuse them away from my table.

Some nights they're here,

others they're there,

but I still can't seem to resist the urge.

Some nights they make me insane,

others they make me feel horrible,

but I still can't seem to get away.

Some nights I imagine what would happen if I fell into their little game.

Then I realize,

if I did,

when they knock,

they would win,

and it would be me who let them in.

I am not beautiful

Maybe to you, but not to me

I am not beautiful

and if I am, I cannot see

I try to think I am gorgeous as can be

but days go by

I look in the mirror

nothing but skin

I cry.

I cry because I am not beautiful

I cry because I don't see what others see

I cry because I *get* eaten alive

by my Insecurities.

I don't know *how* to be beautiful

So I throw on some eyeliner,

 lipstick

and a dress

maybe this costume won't show that I am a mess

I am not beautiful

not one single bit.

If I am,

why can't I tell?

Does the mirror lie?

Or do my eyes deceive me?

I am not beautiful,

maybe to you, but not to me

I am not beautiful,

and if I am, I cannot see.

I am using this pen to write these words on a piece of paper in a note- book my lover bought me.

I am doing this because it helps me.

It helps me ignore all of my depression,

My depression makes me feel crazy.

I get these urges to do things to myself,

Things I promised long ago I'd never do again.

And I never have since.

I am using this pen to write these words on a piece of paper in a notebook my lover bought me.

I am doing this because I don't know what I'd be doing if I weren't.

I don't think I'll ever know.

I'll never know.

I can't do anything right.

So, it seems.

I am doing the best I can.

I am not perfect.

I am not the sheep everyone is trying so hard to be.

I am just *me*

But that is not good enough,

So, it seems...

I can't remember

the last time I had

a real smile on

my face...

depression is funny like that.

When I die, I do not wish to come back.

But when I die, if I do come back

I wish to come back as a big *beautiful* tree.

One with the forest.

One with nature.

When I die, I do not wish to come back.

But when I die, and if I do

A big *beautiful* tree is what I shall be.

I am drowning in my despair.

I cannot save myself.

My lungs fill up

more and more

each day.

And each day gets

longer.

And with each long day,

it gets harder.

Breathing just hurts anymore.

I can keep friends.

Friends just can't keep me.

If I were to show you my back,

Your jaw would drop at the amount

of scars there are.

Don't let those

Beady,

Blood shot

Red eyes

Feed you lies.

For this thing is not your friend.

Even if it tells you

time

and

time

again.

Do not let it take your hand.

It does not love you.

It just wants to

destroy you.

but you don't know that.

Not yet.

I am not really sure what to write...

Not much is on my mind.

I like that though,

it's refreshing.

Like fresh air after a wildfire,

Today I feel like *me*

Today is a good day.

And where do we go from here?

When all that we love is lost

All that we hate is found and I just don't know how we are supposed to make that work with our dysfunctional selves.

It is the little things that count but those little things keep getting lost along the way of this twisted dark trail and can you see it?

What I see?

The light,

where all we are is held but we cannot touch no matter what.

I think this trail is dangerous, but our minds don't seem to care. We know what this is, we are well aware

we just don't know how to fix it.

and we are strong, but we feel weak and those on the outside don't get that, those on the outside keep looking in, they see nothing but the dark they cannot see us because, well we can't even see us.

Anxiety and depression, oh how you love me so.

Leaving me confused, frightened, empty.

How could I resist you?

You make me feel like shit,

Oh, how you love me so.

I'm standing in the middle of my kitchen not sure what the fuck to eat and oh anxiety you make me weak, shaking as I write these words, crying because I don't know what to do with myself

You looked away for a moment, so I grabbed some chips before you could judge me for it,

And depression, my dearest of all how you love me too

Too much might I add. You smother me, and I hate it.

But you love it.

I can feel you scratching my back with those razor blades for nails and I can feel you boring those big beady eyes into the back of my head waiting for the perfect millisecond to feast on my aching soul.

Oh, how you love me so.

She doesn't like the cold

Yet she stands in

your arms

longing for the exchange of words

she has always dreamt to share.

Problem is, she knows your words will remain

untrue.

She doesn't like the cold,

yet she still loves you.

Words are just words

Actions are just actions

Things are just things

Until they are broken then they are more

Broken words are bleeding hearts

Actions are fists in the face instead of the wall

Things are less sentimental than they were when she gave them to you before everything became "more"

Now you question yourself after every text message that reads "I love you, it won't happen again" because words are more important than a text and the words are already broken so how will you ever know what the truth really is?

If she meant it, she would show it and she does so but not how you want her to.

You ask, "is she worth my love?" Your conscience says "no" your heart says "always"

Hers says "forever"

Do

Or

Don't.

I honestly don't care.

It's your life,

Not mine.

Live it how you please.

My mind is blank

I am hungry for entertainment.

Feed me.

My mind is empty.

I just wanted to eat lunch today. I didn't get any further than a quarter way through... By then to me it was disgusting yet it was so delicious.

I just wanted to fill my stomach with dinner. I got maybe half way through then I filled the rest with hate.

I told myself I'm annoying and fat.

I told myself I cannot do a damn thing right.

Maybe I should stop. Maybe I should tell myself I am pretty alright, and maybe then will I be.

But I mean I got depressed. And then I got more so.

At that point at hopped in the shower and cried and just fucking cried. I cried until my eyes went dry.

I just wanted to be happy and stay happy. I don't know what more to do.

I'm fucking sick and tired of being down in the blues

At least I'm working my way through.

It's like being locked inside an isolation cell of a prison,

Only your cuffs have yet to be removed.

It's like being stuck inside of a strait jacket and having a boulder changed to your ankles,

then thrown into the bottom of the Atlantic Ocean from the edge of an Antarctica cliff.

It's like being thrown into a white padded room, only the pads are filled with hollow needles that feel like a brand-new feather pillow poking and pricking at your face

or

that new feather blanket pricking and poking at your body causing you to toss and turn all through the night when all you wanted was a good night's sleep.

It's like a never-ending eclipse.

It's like looking at the face of a 7-year-old little boy who just found out Santa isn't real, or that 5-year-old little girl that just found out she's not getting a pretty pink pony for her 6th birthday in two days.

It's like listening to your mother cry on a repeat playlist on full blast and no matter what you do, you cannot stop it.

It's when you're holding onto a very fragile, frayed thread that's attached to everything you have ever known and loved,

It's when you slowly start to lose your appetite, you don't realize you've begun to starve yourself.

It's when you've been dealing with it for so long, you've finally gone numb.

Those days where you just don't want to exist, I get it.

Yes, they're real days but it doesn't feel like it does it?

It feels like you're in a dream, or a video game. It feels as if you put on a virtual reality headset and got sucked right into it, you know like those movies where they literally go into their video games? Yeah... you know.

It gets annoying because all of a sudden, this giant blue dog is hovering over you, drooling and begging for a bone only the bone it wants is you.

You are nothing but a chewing bone in the eyes of this giant, blue dog.

I suppose I get chewed on a lot because I am usually mentally and physically drained.

I get it though, I do.

I get you, and you.

You are not alone.

She doesn't like to look

in the mirror.

She is afraid of seeing

her reflection.

It is so hard to look at

a face

so sad.

No-one likes that.

Depression has nearly taken over my life, nearly taken all I am and what I stand for.

& I'm like *you're so green*

It's already taken my happiness from me, yet it still comes back for more no matter how many "do not disturb" signs I plaster on my door.

I don't necessarily *want* help, although I know I *need* it.

All I will be told is what I already fucking know.

I mean I've been behind this wheel for a while now and my gas gauge is sitting above E.

Depression. It is taking a toll on me, a toll I cannot pay you see, my wallet is empty

I am running on dry bones and hopeless dreams.

This is not the interstate I wanted to take, and unfortunately enough the next exit is 5 miles down past breakdown Blvd. crossing anxiety street.

I still have to get past this toll, but like I said, I am broke.

Please, Mr. toll-booth-man

can you spare a hand?

Otherwise I may not make it to my destination called 'happiness'

But no,

Of course not.

Depression is the only one running the booth.

I caught myself deep in thoughts.

Deep in thoughts I don't want to be in.

But, as of 1:20 pm on a chilly October afternoon I am knee deep in these thoughts. As if I thought these thoughts, I am thinking couldn't get worse.

As the tide begins to rise, it rises higher and higher sending unnerving chills up my thighs,

I stand there hyperventilating, trying to relax but my airways are beginning to close up, my lungs need air and I am so dizzy *so why am I covering my mouth with a wash rag?*

The thoughts get stronger, my brain is thinking of ways I can do it and places I can(t) hide it, depression continues to hover over me like a dark rain cloud full of electricity ready to strike!

Suddenly my conscious kicks in and I can breathe again. I stand there, and I stare at my reflection until the tears fade away.

The tide has gone down, the cloud has faded away.

I caught myself thinking of actions left unsaid.

I caught myself thinking...

I caught myself;

Shitty feelings lead to shitty thoughts and shitty thoughts lead to cups full of tears and cups full of tears leads to baths full of blood and baths full of blood lead to heart aches and heart breaks. But if those tears don't turn to blood, they just turn to bricks instantly putting up a wall to anyone who tries to dry the tears up, the problem is I'm drowning in them and if this wall keeps building its self-higher and higher, how much longer will I be able to keep my head up? If a door isn't made anytime soon, how much longer will I be able to breathe?

Take care!

Thanks, I will!

I don't.

I skip meals, I don't wash my hair for days at a time, I don't lotion my body knowing my skin is extra sensitive come winter time. I smile when I feel like crying a river and I criticize each and everything I do.

I don't take care of me. I don't see a point. But sometimes I let myself sink a little too deep and when I realize that I do

I come back to the surface again.

I never know for how long. I just take advantage.

It's like this annoying waiting game and most days it's very intense then by night I just want to sleep. Even that's a hard task to do.

Are you okay?

Yes, I am, thanks!

I'm not.

I bottle up my emotions as if my soul is empty as if they have no matter being here - because that's how it feels anyways. I cry myself to sleep when I can't sleep at all then I tear myself to bits and pieces.

I'm not even sure what I am supposed to do anymore. I help myself as much as I possibly can, but most of the time I need a hand.

Though lately it seems like I've been needing a life jacket.

I do not understand why this depression lies over me with the weight of a soaking wet blanket, but it does.

I am already cold enough and the heater is up to 75 yet, my body is still forming goose bumps.

I would like to feel the heat at some point, the sun doesn't shine here often in the winter time and when it does it still isn't enough; the air is cold, and the wind is only making it worse and all I want to do is enjoy a walk before it rains again.

I did my best.

The best I could; to shine brighter than the sun did today, but I met only half that goal.

I suppose half way is better than no way at all.

Someday I might just meet that goal, someday may also never come.

I read that the best part about life is having the ability to live, not to suffer... When will I get a chance to "live" again?

I never understood those commercials about the little spin up dude with the lady that would wind him up just for him to slump down again. I always thought it was something about back pain, I knew it was about being sad... Not why.

I never understood the commercial where the guy wakes up sad, does everything sad until he entered the real world then one day... Disappeared. Still.... Why?

I never understood the word depression or even the fact that it has a family.

Growing up I didn't get a lot of things....

I didn't get why I couldn't understand but I could feel.

Silly, I know, being young and knowing sad

Being outgoing and knowing anxiety.

I never understood depression... What it was.

I wish I didn't now.

Silly growing up to learn of things you don't yet understand. Still feeling. Still not knowing.

When I was young, I would rip little small pieces of hair out of my head. Other times it wasn't little Sally Lou who bit my hand to the point of breaking skin in the classroom or on the playground.

It was me.

I'd learned to cope with my emotions by self-harm at a young age. Yet I didn't know that.

No one told me about that, I never saw it, nor did anyone I knew do it.

I just did it as if it were some type pf second nature. And as I got older, I began to understand.

I also learned that a razor blade could do more than cut open a box.

I wish I had understood that I wasn't a box.

Whenever we would go out to eat, and I'd run out of napkins or need a drink refill, "just wave the wait or down when you see 'em" is what I hear so as soon as I see that waiter I shove my face full of food then make awkward eye contact leaving the person I am with to ask the favor for me.

When we would go to the store, I try to walk furthest away from the checkout lane... You really think my anxiety wants to talk to Linda over there?

... He thinks not.

I never understood being "shy", I never understood why Latuda was a thing for sadness, what depression meant. I never knew what an anxiety attack was. I never knew what it meant to lose yourself, yet everyone can around still see you. .... I wish I never did.

Tired of waking up not knowing what to do with myself, let alone my day. Tired of being woken by my depression tired of not being able to sleep because of it too. Tired of feeling like I'm not good enough I just am so sick of it, is it blood that you want? Blood you cannot get? I will not sit here and continue to chew on razors to please you I cannot handle this pain any longer you are running me dry and no matter how much water I drink I just cannot seem to get enough, I cannot handle this. I cannot handle you. But I will not give up.

I don't know when I'll get a break from this soul crushing depression but I'm sick of it. I'm sick of having to take advantage of moments of happiness to feel happy for even at least just 10 seconds. I love the feeling of feeling. When it's a good feeling. These bad feeling and these wild emotions aren't so good and at times I feel like I'm stuck in a strait jacket. My depression has drug me so far and pulled me in so deep I don't know how to cope.

When I break, I break hard and I don't even know why, can't I just have a day just one, please oh please? I'm sick of wallowing in sadness I'm tired of feeding my insecurities please oh please my demons just let me free let me be. I can't bare this being prisoner any longer and I've fought for so long I've taken the whips of your leather and chains, I've starved because of your negative words and I've bled so much, for so long it began to terrify me. I'm so scared, I just want to be happy again.

I want to be myself again, I want to feel the feeling of a true genuine smile that I shouldn't have had to steal away from you though it's my smile, so maybe you're the one who stole it in the first place. Fuck you. I just want happiness. I just want freedom.

Oh, how divine it must be, to live in a world such as thee, to not lack a good dose of happy, oh how divine it must be.

I'm not sure about you, but me? Even the slightest of laughter brings a smile to my face, and in that smile is a new path waiting to be used. A path that allows me to be happy,

And behind that happy is me, really me... The me that is really, happy.

And as divine as it must be, I know it won't last

So, I make the best of it, the best that I can. Because sometimes my happy comes a little too late. .... Oh, how divine it must be.

Some days it's just me. Well most days. Ha. Okay that isn't funny but it's true. I'd like to have some company though, no matter how much my depression refuses it. Some days it's just me and my thoughts and my thoughts run wild and suddenly I'm having an anxiety attack over the same word that keeps rotating around my soggy brain and it drives me insane to feel this way it drives me mad to be alone it drives me off the edge to be lonely and to be lonely well.... It's not something to be at all but when you are it doesn't make a difference how many warm bodies are surrounding you it doesn't matter how much those bodies care, or how much they listen or how many times they repeat the words "I love you" it does not matter because that loneliness is still there and it is the only thing you can feel and the shitty part is how cold it is, it's so cold and that's the only comfort you get, those warm bodies cannot make enough warmth for that loneliness to thaw away. I like my alone time, but I don't like to be lonely, not one bit, not one. single. fucking. bit. My loneliness is often accompanied by my utterly ruthless depression.

Most days it's just me, my depression and I.

Most days, I'm just lonely

But I'll always know, I am not alone.

My depression has turned into anger. I mean, before it was just depression with a light annoyance but now? When depression walks through my door, unannounced usually he would slam the door behind him. Lately though, he's been sneaking in and creepin' a friend, a fiend to me, he is no luxury. He is small and hot, he is loud and submissive, and he knows no fear.

Lately, depression has been sneaking anger into my home, allowing him to my room and jump on my bed, while depression "sings" me his own lullabies all the while anxiety is turning my home onto an earthquake. I do not want this, I sometimes wish they would abide by what rules they read. I mean my fence says, "no trespassing" and my front door holds a "no solicitors" sign .... So why, why, fucking WHY has my guard dog fallen shy? I built these walls to my home a long time ago, then I put a lock on my fence, and I'd hoped and wished it would never open again, but it did. And I lost the key. So now I'll never know who's bombarding in on me or when or even how. I can't even remember the last time I sat comfortably on my own couch let alone the last time I could lie my head comfortably on my own bed, or when my pillow didn't kink my neck. I can't remember the last time I enjoyed a meal without painting on a fake smile let alone feeling a real smile flutter upon my cheeks. My depression has been acting up lately. It's been whispering in my ears, things I don't want to hear.

My depression is no laughing matter, though he finds himself quite amusing; as his friends do too.

Been waking up depressed every day for the past month.

And every day for the past month I've wanted to die.

But really, do I?

I'm so unhappy, I don't know why

But I know when I look up there is blue in the sky

A blue that much matches mine.

In this state you get grey clouds and dark skies

Lately it's been bright

But something doesn't feel right.

Every day for the past month I've been dragging two 2-ton weights at my feet

I don't want to do anything

Yet I yearn to do everything.

Just something,

Something nice.

A simple hike

Or fly a kite.

(I don't know how to fly kites.)

Today I am glad the sun is shining again,

Today I am glad it will be 76 degrees

Today I am sad

I wonder when I'll start to shine again

Lately I've been shining with a dim light

I try

I try

I try...

And then I do nothing but cry.

I do not have the energy to even crack a smile

The last swig of a warm Corona,

The shot of patron chased by tequila.

That is me... Not so great; but worth it.

Room temperature pizza and a flat soda,

That is me... Gross; but something.

A worn-down quilt with holes in it,

That is me... Broken down; but warm and comfortable.

A poem, written terribly,

That is me... Crumbled up; but never torn apart.

I hold my head high, with confidence filling my aura, love and laughter radiating from me. Yet something is missing, just a little piece and that piece is happiness. I hold my head high to ward off any evil, yet it feels so weighed down by this devil called depression.

I used to fear monsters under my bed, even so the supposed ones in my closet; then I grew up. The monsters I am now most afraid of are the ones in my brain, the ones who have told me it is ohkay to go insane, that it is ohkay to lose faith and that it is ohkay to lose hope.

The same monsters who told me all my pain would disappear with slit of a silver blade. I wish I knew, I wish I knew that not to be true. Every day I see my scars and every day I wish I'd not touched that shit.

Every day I wish I were stronger,

every day I wish I would have not let me get the best of me. Now I've got to live with this thing, I feel like I am my own worst enemy, this thing I cannot say his name much like Beetlejuice you say it not two, but three times and he appears out of fucking nowhere really. I hold my head high, with confidence, laughter and love but happiness is what I yearn for, I hold my head high in hopes that one day, happiness may drive by and decide to park in my empty space.

See I used to fear monsters under my bed, until I started learning about the ones living in my head and I'll tell you what, it's a fucking bitch. I wish someone would have told me the god damn truth. I wish someone would have prepared me for the real monsters. I wish someone would have really done something about my bullies. I wish someone would have noticed I started hating myself when I was five. Now I'm twenty and I don't even know what self-love is.

I don't know what confidence is.

I hardly recognize happiness when she comes around.

Happiness isn't easy to find, nor is it easy to get and sometimes it seems as if it is too expensive. Happiness is a necessity a necessity that I cannot get my hands on and I don't want to live my life with my head down but sometimes I just crash, and I cannot recover.

Sometimes I just worry, and I cannot stop. Sometimes I just cry, and I cry, and I cry until my tears are gone and eyes are dried. Sometimes I wish I could just disappear from the world for a bit, to find myself all over again. Sometimes I wish I just didn't exist.

I must remind myself, every day that I am loved and needed and wanted by most. And every day I have to tell myself I matter because sometimes those words from others aren't as strong as when I say it myself. So, I do. And maybe that's just it but even when I do so,

I don't believe the words from my own mouth. Is that me or my depression speaking? I don't know anymore. I am just so sick and fucking tired of this god damn war.

I feel pretty and confident today.

I've been waiting all week to feel this.

I feel beautiful and that makes my heart warm and joyful

I think I am pretty today, most days I don't feel this way. I mask my insecurities and do my best to look beautiful but deep down I feel gross and my insecurities pick and pick and pick at me until I finally break that mask.

Not today; today I feel beautiful.

It seems as if the days are getting longer and slower, sometimes I feel like it's just my mind playing tricks on me. Could it be? Maybe. Either way, I wish it'd stop. I am becoming bored of this; I am losing motivation.

I wish I could just sit and not think for once, not about a thing. Oh, how pleasant that would be.

I get bored of listening to myself on repeat. It doesn't make my days any better.

It seems as if I am shutting down, becoming a closed book all over again. Slowly but surely. I am just tired of flipping the pages.

Perhaps,

I am just tired **...**

I've always wondered what it was like, to you know taste the lips that belong to death.... Just for a moment, not for an eternity.

A moment, sir just a second of your time is all I need.

It's all I need to feel, something. Just one thing. Just.... Anything.

I'm so numb lately even a blade wouldn't make me feel a thing. Not anymore. Not again.

But you, you are so much stronger, sharper and more peaceful than anything could possibly be.

I've always wondered what it would be like, to you know look into deaths dark hollow eyes and allow him to take in my soul in and let it back out.

A moment, sir just a second of your time is all I need.

If you don't mind, do this favor for me.

I need to feel something, anything.

Sir, please.

And someday this will all be over. I won't lose hope and I'll hold on to the little bit of faith I have left, in myself and the universe. I will stay strong no matter how hard it is to stand, I will never be able to fly if I never learn to walk. And the day I learn to walk will be the day I learn to fly because if anything, I deserve that much. I've been stuck here for a while, wallowing in my sorrow; it's time to throw that out the window. When I think of myself being happy, I think of a better life, I think of a better future and I think of a better world. Is it too much to ask to be left alone? Is it too much to ask my depression to walk away? Is it too much to ask for a real smile to form upon my face? I wouldn't think it is, I just think it takes a lot of courage. A lot of courage that I don't have. A lot of courage to muck up. But I promise myself, I will do just that. I will go to the ends of the earth and back times 2 to make sure I have my happy ending. The end may be far from here, but happiness is not. And happiness is what I yearn to achieve. So, hear me now, hear me whisper "I am happy" and then I'll scream to the top of my lungs with joy, why? Because I will finally be happy. I will finally be able to smile. I will finally be... Me all over again.

Until then, I'll enjoy the view from here.

1,200 calories a day.

1,200 left to go.

9 am.... She cleans the house, ignoring her stomachs screams for food.

1,200 left to go.

12 pm

Her stomach grumbles and she's losing her balance as if she just downed a 12 pack.

Her emotions aren't working well with her today.

12:20 pm

She eats.

Something small, not too much though. That's too risky.

1,000 left to go.

12:30 pm

She reads her book, it's interesting, but not so interesting that she forgets about purging.

The toilet is calling her name.

She grabs her book mark.

1,200 left to go.

3 pm

She hates herself. But she hates her disorder even more.

She's too hard on herself, she weighs 100.5 lbs. but that is just not enough.

1,200 left to go.

5 pm

Dinner is done. It's time to eat but she can hardly stand on her own two feet.

The thought of this dinner, the smell so good yet so wretched.

Her mouth waters but her head says "stop." She heads for the stairs but cannot bring herself to walk down.

1,200 left to go.

6 pm

She's making her way down and into the kitchen, it took her long enough just staring at the stairs knowing what will be awaiting her after she eats.

A plate of spaghetti. It's her favorite dish.

She piles it up, takes advantage of her randomly happy mood.

700 left to go.

6:30pm

The toilet. Again.

1,000 left to go. 9 pm

She lies in bed. She skipped the shower, but she didn't skip the water or bottle of pills her father forgot on the counter.

9:10 she thinks

9:15 she contemplates

9:20 she stares at the lid

9:45 she twists it off

10:00 she is out cold.

......

1,200 calories a day.

1,200 left to go.

8 am

Her father is in tears, the ambulance has arrived. He hopes and wishes he got to her in time. 'It's too late, too late.'

12:15 pm

She was pronounced dead.

All she ever strived to be was perfect and skinny.

1,200 was just 1 too many.

250 calories and... Not really counting.

Breakfast was enough, that late evening snack was more than so.

She's not sure anymore. Why does she do this to herself?

So, she wonders, and she never really notices the affect this disorder has on her.

She hardly even considers it a disorder.

So please, she begs.

Please. Don't worry about me.

The words slide out smooth like the silk dress that falls from her skin bone hips at night when she tries and tries to please her eyes with the view of her fragile body.

But to her, it is a body that needs to lose more.

To her, it is not skin and bones but fat and cellulite.

250 calories and now counting.

Though, the calories are not rising they are declining.

And once she finds her way to that public restroom again...

0 calories... No more counting.

I wonder what it's like to wake up every morning feeling happy or feeling nothing at all, but never numb. I am curious to know how it feels to smile and really mean it, not just because someone said you need to smile more. Sometimes I wonder what it would be like to be free. Free of so many things; dreadful things. Because painting a god damn smile on your face every time you wake up or every time you just relax is really fucking exhausting and quite frankly, I don't want to deal with this shit anymore. I am running out of my shade of pink anyways. So, what's the use? Why waste the last drop of paint on a fake smile when I can just use it on a canvas?

I wonder, every day. Curious as can be, hopefully someday I will see the light that is supposed to shine from beneath me. And maybe someday I will be happy.

I will be me.

I think I was pretty content with O.C.D and self-hatred.
That was easy to ignore.

But then life had to happen the way life has to and depression crept up on me
anxiety tailed behind and needless to say it has really opened my mind,
but I know without it, would be quite divine.
I am soft, and sensitive.

Some days I can't even take a simple joke without getting a little hurt.
But that's just me and I didn't ask to be this way
I just ignore it to the best of my ability.

It's not always easy. It's actually really damn hard
and no matter how many times someone says to me "you're strong
I still have a hard time believing it
because I do not feel as strong as they say.

I feel as if the days will never end

and when they do,
they never seem to stay away for long,
I wish I could just sleep for days
and days and just escape the world we live in.
I wish I could just live in a dream for a while,
just something to get away from this illness.

.. I need a break.

My mind seems to be in other places lately. Like, consciously I am here but really, I'm not. I mean I can't even remember what I did 5 seconds before brushing my teeth. And I don't mean literally five seconds but... Ya know.

It seems as if I have got to snap myself back into reality. I kind of just go into my own world like a dream only it's not a dream nor a day dream. It's just *like* a dream.

When I say it's like a dream, I mean it's like a world I would rather be in because there it is peaceful and by peaceful, I mean people-less and by people-less I mean only filled with people I love, and people who love me.

I mean, I like it. Don't get me wrong but I also like being here. I just don't love it, no but it's better than being alone.

I do not treat myself the way I should.

So instead, I tell myself I deserve nothing.

I do not treat my body well.

So, I call it fat.

I treat my emotions as if they do not matter.

So, I shut them out.

I put a fake smile on my face.

So, when anyone asks, I say "I'm fine"

I treat myself as if I am not skinny enough

So, I feed my body less.

I treat my life as if it does not matter.

So, I take sharp turns on the back road like a jackass.

I have a lot of self-hate.

And love is all I want to give to myself.

How do I do that if I have never been taught how?

She doesn't know how to control her thoughts any more.

Lately she doesn't even remember the last thing she ate or watched on TV.

Some days she feels so lost, like she's been here before, but something just doesn't click.

She's been going through a never-ending maze and this maze is really getting boring.

She can't handle this puzzle any longer. She keeps hearing "you're getting stronger" but she cannot believe it.

So, she bothers not to push herself but to give up she can't think of a reason to keep going.

She gives up.

Pulls out a little sharp silver thing.

She gave up.

She grazed that little silver thing across her arm with no hesitation.

She just couldn't do it.

I am merely a closed book. And I do not open up to really anyone. Not if I don't want to because 95% of the time I'm chained and locked anyhow.

Quite frankly I do not care, I've spent so much time being a closed book that I just settle on the page I'm reading, and I just let it be. Most of the time I won't open my book for a long while, my story gets boring and I really don't have the patience to wait for the excitement. So.... I keep my book closed. Locked and chained. Key thrown far, far away. Maybe the rain will make the words spread and I won't have to read it again.

I scare myself though, when I don't open up. I hold in this climax to my story, the part where I get overwhelmed and I feel useless and all I want to do is curl up in a ball and cry and wish I could just fucking rot and die!

I scare myself because these thoughts become so suppressed that I search for the nearest sharp object and I hold it to any part; any place of my skin and I try and try to muck up the courage to once again alter my skin.

But I can't, I just cannot because I go back to three years and 11 months ago to when I promised you, I would never commit such an action again. And I remind myself how not worth it the aftermath is. And suddenly I will be fine.

I put the sharp object away. So, it can wait to be used for what it's made.

Altering skin is not it.

I let my chains hang loose and I try my best to open my book up for you.

So, you can hold me and comfort me and remind me that my story is merely a bad dream.

I know better

Yet I still allow these thoughts to consume me

These beauty standards

They are so

Low.

Yet I still allow them to bully me.

My body is not big

Yet I still seem to think I need to lose more weight

I am much smarter

Though I dumb myself down enough to allow these photoshopped pizzas to get to me

They look like super models

Its fucking pizza.

Yet, I'm over here crying because I don't look like a fucking photoshopped pizza

I am so beautiful

But I still tell myself I am not.

I know better

Yet I still count my calories

I starve myself for days at a time.

I eat too much.

No.

I don't eat enough.

You know, I actually just

Fucking give up.

Just because I am a closed book does not mean my feelings should go unnoticed. Yes of course, I get nervous when asked "are you ohkay?" Especially in front of a room full of other people; yes, the only two people across the room who can't even hear you count as a room full of people.

Why? My anxiety says so.

Does that mean I don't want to be checked on? No, it just means to please ask me quietly, perhaps write it down on a paper or text it to me real fast. I'll be sure to answer I just need some help here.

Just because I won't unlock the chains that guard my pages from being seen, does not mean I am pushing you or anyone else away, I am just simply afraid that if I vent then my feelings will not matter and if I vent, I may be looked at as if I am begging for attention and though I know you are aware that I am not, I am still afraid.

That being said, if you could just kindly hold my hand or perhaps hug me, that would be fine. I just want to be held most of the time.

Most of the time I want to be told everything will be ohkay because even when I know it won't, it's gotta be at some point.

And at some point, if it is not, well that's alright... I mean it's going to have to be.

But just know, that because I am a closed book that does not mean to dismiss my obvious feelings.

Just hug me....

Hold me....

Whisper in my ear that everything is going to be alright....

Hug me all day

And if you have to,

Please...

Hold me all night. .

I enjoy these days where I can soak up the sun and the heat it spits out. It feels like happiness. I love that feeling. It feels like purity. I enjoy the feeling of the sun, the ever so gentle kisses it leaves on my shoulders.

I enjoy these days when I can enjoy the true purity of real happiness and that it was matters the most to me right now. Today, I was happy... Truly happy and tomorrow I hope I will be today.

I enjoy these days where I can sit by the water and listen to it while it dances under the clouds and reflects the blue sky. Its calming, relaxing.

I enjoy days like these. .

The world is blind.

And no one can see that.

Because no one wants to open their eyes to see a land that was once so beautiful turn to dust.

No one wants to open their eyes and see that in fact, the earth is falling apart beneath our feet and the sand is trickling between our toes

Its so soft and brings so much comfort until we see we are standing on nothing... Nothing but hatred, hurt, abuse, loneliness, madness, desperation

And I am nothing but desperate to fix this

Because in the next ten years I want to see big beautiful pine trees soaring taller than a skyscraper

I want to see the flowers blooming

I want to see the birds singing and the squirrels playing chicken because all they wanted was their acorns

I want to see the next generation know the color green in its true and purest form

I want to see my future children come home and tell me about the big ol' dandelions they see in the grass or how a giant blue butterfly landed on their nose

I want to see animals live in love, not in fear.

I want to see more abandoned land recreated so that way we don't have to continue to tear down what's hardly left.

The world is blind to its own selfish needs, no one ever stopped to actually smell the roses. Instead they picked them.

Instead, they let them rot on their counters in a cup of water.

Instead, they let green fade to brown. And suddenly, everything was black. .

I really hate how ignorant and closed-minded people can be to depression. They expect us to cheer up and smell the roses as if we who are depressed are not trying hard enough.

I mean come on, if you are going to tell us how to be happy then take a damn minute to learn of this illness we suffer from before you give us your opinion. We want facts.

It is not what you think it is.

Depression is not just going to bed early so you're not so tired the next day

It's more like "oh hey its 9:30 I'm going to go lay down for bed" then the moment you close your eyes your mind is like "hey kid remember that time..." And all the memories come flooding back,

image by image

Scene by scene.

So now, you have turned the TV back on.

Switch on the light.

And just wait to fall asleep in hopes your memories don't haunt your dreams.

Depression is not just being a fat ass and needing to eat a salad

It's more like "man, I am really sad... Maybe some comfort food will help." It also isn't needing a burger or two it's more like looking in the mirror and your eyes are like 'wow... Dude your stomach... It just like... Jiggled a bit, you're fat bro'

It's like, seeing is believing and your eyes can be deceiving.

Depression is not just being compulsive and going insane. It's more like what else besides this blade can take away my pain?

Depression is not just being addicted to a video game or website

It's more like I need a distraction before relapsing.

It is not just being lazy and sitting on your ass doing nothing to help yourself

It's more like "hey I have these weights on my shoulders and my feet are dragging boulders across this quick sand and I really need some help, I am just too weak to hold my hand out"

Depression is a tunnel in hell.

Depression is an isolation cell.

And no matter how much it seems we don't need help

.

.

9 times out of ten we are silently screaming for it.

You just have to listen for us.

Because sometimes we need YOU to reach out.

It isn't always so simple being so strong.

Stressed and depressed. And you may not see this, that I am not reaching out for help.

I am screaming but the thing is these walls are thick and my doors are locked, my ceiling will not cave in, due to worries that I will escape, and I am not in the proper mental state to really actually care about this when and where type of shit. So, I am sorry to anyone who actually tries to help I feel like I am just broken beyond repair, I am broken so I just sit there.

Stressed and depressed. I am dreaming. Dreaming of a place and time that happiness will walk up to me and finally shake my hand again, "welcome, please... Do come in" with open arms and wide smiles.

As for now, I do all I can... It tears me down and as cliché as I may say; I get back up again.

Stressed and depressed. A lifelong test, a test I fear I will fail. A test I feel I have taken over and over again maybe I just need a better teacher, maybe I need a better leader, maybe I need to clear my head proper, maybe I need to lay in bed longer? Though if I do so, I might as well not get back up because the funds for a better teacher are really not enough.

but, please oh please I really need her.

I cannot stay this way in pain as such as the pain I feel, it is so surreal.

The bubbles on this answer sheet are too small, no too blurry? Oh no, I'm going to fail again... I better scurry.

I'm out teacher, I cannot do this any longer. I'm dropping out this class, I'm tired of reminiscing my past. .

I'm tired of being tired, so I have become angry.

But I am growing tired of anger and now I don't know what to do.

If I'm not tired, I'm angry if I'm not angry I'm tired and by tired,

I mean sad and by sad,

I mean depressed and by depressed,

I mean I want to take a razor to every inch of my fucking skin,

but I just cannot, so I cry and cry and cry until the pain and the urges slide away.

It takes a while though, for it to leave.

I walk back and forth to the general sharp object area fighting every nerve I have to make sure I don't even look at it.

I refrain myself then I become mad and by mad

'

I mean angry and by angry,

I mean I just want to throw this chair at the fucking window and shatter everything in sight,

I want to cause random destruction and get in a physical fight.

I want to scream and shout I want to let it all out but where do I go where no one will know?

If I am actually alone, I am afraid of what I might do.

And I'm so tired of feeling bad about something when I shouldn't because I held every fucking right to be the way I was. So, fuck you. And fuck these emotions.

Fuck me too.

I'm tired of feeling these feelings I feel.

I envy happiness in its purity because happiness is a goal I feel I am struggling to achieve. .

My rebound words are "I'm fine" if they aren't that shallow lie that says "I'm ohkay" but I suppose if that's what I say that's what I am but really, it's not. Shallow words have hollow meanings. You asked me "are you ohkay?" I respond "I'm fine" but really, I'm not. And you know that, but you don't push for the real answer after asking a second time.

I appreciate that.

Instead you look at me with that concerned face and when I look down you make a silly sound, I look up to see what it is and you're there with your arms out and lips puckered up I step closer.

That's all i need. That's all i silently ask for. And you know it so well and I don't know how but you just do, i guess it's just like how i know you.

So, thank you, I appreciate it and I know I don't need to thank you because apparently that's your job, to make me feel better and to feel loved. To make me feel less alone and you distract me from these contradicting thoughts... really, I couldn't be more grateful.

To have someone such as you in my life. That... that is something. So, when my words are shallow, and I lie when saying I'm just fine, continue to do what you do... because baby, it works every time

I'm sorry.

I know I have worn those words to the ground, and I know I say it too much and I'm sorry for that.... shit... I'm sorry... damnit.... Look I can't help it, really.

I try to refrain myself from saying it, but I always feel like I owe an apology for something,

you can just blame that one on my anxiety.

And I know it is frustrating as it is to hear me repeat "I'm sorry" then apologizing for apologizing because you said I don't have a reason to apologize.

So, I'm sorry.

I did it again... I know... it's just so hard not to do so.

If anything, please just accept it because that's all I really want. I know I don't *have* to apologize but I do it anyways because my anxiety says so. Otherwise I might just cry... not because of you or because you won't accept my unnecessary apology but simply because anxiety told me I'm a terrible person for not apologizing for bumping into your door frame.... as if I need to apologize for being clumsy but that's just me.

So, I'm sorry, really.

To smile in your face while lying that I'm ohkay would be a shot to the heart for both you and I because it is more painful to keep this depression in than it is to let it out and when you can clearly tell I am most definitely not alright you can see my mind is not at ease and neither are my hands or my feet.

I'm trying to distract myself and I'm looking at the old cobwebs in the corner of the boat rather than looking at the grey clouds in the blue sky and you say my name time after time, but I don't reply until maybe the ninth time you've repeated it

I know I seem distant a lot and I'm not trying to be I'm just wallowing in depression and suffocating in pity

I shame myself for having this mental illness when I know I shouldn't, but I don't care anymore, and it probably doesn't help much.

Lately my head space has been filled with "what ifs" and "why's" I've been questioning myself...

My sanity to be exact

because I get these fucked up thoughts and they seem so real so when they feel real,

I wonder what would happen if I made the thought come to life but that wouldn't be a good idea,

especially not for my sake and it scares me.

A lot.

It does.

I feel like a failure and I feel like that's all I'll ever be.

What if I don't stop feeling these feelings?

Or thinking these thoughts?

What if I go off the rails, would I still be loved?

Would I be missed?

But why would I think of things like this?

I cannot fathom the thought of taking my own life especially from others.

Why can't I think like a normal human being?

Or deal with things like a regular person?

Why do I have to over think a situation and then break down over it or have an anxiety attack?

The thoughts I hold in my brain scare me, they make me feel like I'm going insane.

I can no longer take this mental pain...

Every day I wake up I paint a smile upon my face, and no one can tell whether it is real or fake so that way no one has to ask me if I am ohkay, I have mastered the arts of painting a fake smile to look so real. I don't know where this will end, hell I hardly know where it begins and I honestly and truly wish this life would end but I don't want it to be over so soon I have yet to get to the climax of my story, I'd like to know where this adventure goes but it is hard to continue walking through mud and quick sand all it does is slows me down and suddenly I begin to frown... Maybe if I stop going, I'll just slowly drown as my lungs begin turning into a sandbox on a children's playground I mean I am already suffocating slowly but surely. I'd like to just go now... But where is there to go when I cannot escape what is inside my desperate brain? .

My depression has been sleeping over a lot. I told him he wasn't welcome here, he didn't listen.

He doesn't care, he just looks at me and stares boring those black filled eyes into my skin burning my flesh layer by layer.

I have been so depressed I stepped on a Lego and even that didn't hurt.

Needless to say, I've been numb... And very lost... I can't even remember what happened yesterday... Shit I don't remember my drive to work this morning.

Honestly, I just don't want to exist anymore there's no reason behind my depression a lot of the time. At least if I know it's easier but lately, I don't know, and it just lingers.

I wish I could make this mental pain go away I am so afraid of these thoughts in my brain telling me to do this or do that... These tasks are toxic.

I'd like to just breathe and achieve a real feeling of happiness or manage to crack a real smile for once.

I'm lost.... I'm so depressed. .

I've been wearing a smile on my face as if it's the new fashion trend, lately it seems to be getting some attention so when I am asked if I am alright, I say I am fine, I am great. The words get bought so I continue to sell them as if they're true. Really, they're not. If I were to tell you I am fine, then I would have to talk more, and I do not want to talk more. I want to just be alone, but really, I don't. What I want is to be able to truthfully say I feel like shit. That I feel as if the world would be fine if I just vanished. I want to break down and sob and scream and I just can't... I can't!

Even if I could I probably wouldn't.

I wish a smile would find its way to my face. I wish happiness would find its way to my brain.

I wish this depression would find its way out.

Maybe if I just go to sleep, I wouldn't have to worry about it.

Though... Sometimes it finds its way to my dreams.

I often wonder what it'd be like to be a bird, to freely fly and soar above all that is low

I wonder what it would be like to be free of this jailor.

But he only wants what's best for him, he benefits and grows from my pain and consent is not in his dictionary, the word "no" or "please, just fucking leave" are unheard of. It's as if he is creating a show for his cousins who walk with him hand in hand with a smile upon their face, a smile made up of all the lives they have stolen and all the happiness they have torn out from the owners leaving us with nothing but loneliness, sadness and pain.

I'm in my own cell yet I am still cuffed, he won't unlock these metal rings until I begin to lose more of my brain and go insane and attempt to inflict pain upon my skin... Only then is when he will remove them.

I am trapped, it feels as if I cannot even muster the slightest of a laugh because that considers a smile and smile is what I do not have

And no matter how many times I beg and I plea, no matter how much I ask nicely he pays me no mind and lights up that disgusting cigarette of his.

Sure... You're winning now, Mr. Depression... But for how long?

That is my only question. .

So many triggers and they're all being pulled at the same time

I don't know how long I'll be able to stay inside this insane mind,

I think it's about time I step out of line,

this road to happiness is backed up and this motherfucker thinks he's about to lap up on me and block me from any type of happy,

but that's ohkay you'll see, while you just swoop on in Imma slip right out and take another route,

one I don't doubt you'll get lost on, though I know you'll find your way around. I know who you are, and I know what you are so why don't I go ahead and say it, so you can come on up and face it?

This pain I can't handle any longer ma I can't take it...

I'll make it or I'll break it but there ain't no way I can stay, and I promise I won't do nothing rash, but I like disobeying the speed laws, I like going fast

it puts my mind at ease it takes me to a place I wish I could really be, and I don't see it being any other way....

I'm coming up on a sharp turn and if I don't swerve, I'll brake. I don't want to brake. I don't want to stay in this place I was put into,

I do not want to masquerade my frown in this fucking town, but I am bound to relapse and if I relapse what will I have? What will I be? How will you and he see me?

This line is too damn long. I'll take an alternate route.

The shots have been fired,

the clips have run out.

I am afraid

I am afraid of a lot but mostly I am afraid of rejection,

I am afraid my efforts will be turned down and I won't ever make it

I've dreamt of becoming famous since I was a little girl only,

I saw myself being a singer as most young girls do

come to realize I really can't sing all too well,

but I can write like no other.

Maybe that's because I've always been good at writing my feelings

and when I discovered poetry it became my cherry on top,

my way of being indirect with validation.

I've always seen myself in the spot light singing my heart out but now?

I'd rather be in the spot light holding back the tears

I can feel forcing themselves out as I read this poem about depression and self-doubt out loud.

Meanwhile I'm allowing my thoughts to consume me,

but I thought writing them down and reading them in an angry manner would stop that from happening and maybe it never will, and I don't know if I'll be able to handle that, but I can try at the least.

I can attempt to force a smile no one will have to question.

I can also attempt to stop these hungry thoughts from consuming me.

.

I am not a slave, yet I find myself questioning my sanity over this depression I just so happen to be chained up for.

I have led myself to believe that he treats me right and won't let me down though he does every single day.

Every single day, I silently break. I tear myself apart, I shred my skin like cheese on a grater, I bash my head in like a punching bag in a boxing room, I tell myself awful things... and I feel so translucent.

The key is right there in front of my face, I have yet to lift a finger. Why can't I just grab it and run away?

I am not a slave I just so happen to be addicted to this game; a fucked-up version of life. I am so afraid of failure, I am scared shitless of judgement but then I think again, and I mean... who isn't

sure, there will be critique on anything we possibly do, including breathing. Sure, there will be haters and fakers and heart breakers

Well you know what

Fuck 'em because all you're going to do is get better and you can step right over them, look back and say,

"I told you so"

You have nothing to prove to anyone but you because you are the only person you need to prove a damn thing to.

The key is here, in my hand... all I need to do is unlock these chains.

I am not a slave.

I ruin everything

I wish I could do just one thing right.

Or maybe I don't ruin anything, and I am just ruining myself by destroying my brain with bombarding thoughts of self-harm and death.

I'm too much of a coward to do anything about it.

Self-destruction is probably the worst thing you could bring upon yourself, yet it is so simple to do.

I am such a coward I sit here and allow my depression to bully me and anxiety to kick me in the ribs every twenty seconds.

I am such a coward I feel lost without a sharp object when I'm breaking down.

I am such a coward I rip my happiness away the moment it grazes my shielded heart.

I am such a coward I don't allow help to find me nor I find help because I am afraid I won't be able to write anymore but there is so much more to write about than these silly demons,

There is much more to explore than giving my demons the pleasure of being the spot light of my poetry.

This just so happens to be a simple outlet for me to run away from the darkness consuming me.

I am afraid of so many things and that makes me pretty cowardly.

I am such a coward I went online to search for a therapist and 'forgot' to email them.

Maybe I'm too afraid of help because I am too afraid of judgement as I am with everything else

.

What I would do to feel "normal" for once,

to not have a care in the world

to be able to feel like the world is not watching my every move

to be able to kick anxiety to the curb in order to make those feelings go away

Oh, what I would do;

A fighter. I am that.

Strong. That I am.

Brave. Indeed.

So now, it is time to start believing those things.

Now it is time to start learning how to love myself

holding in this self-hate... So much of it too it continues to stack this unnecessary weight on my shoulders and all this pain, all these worries all this sadness I'm in over my head.

But I've got to admit, it is pretty damn sad how I can't seem to love myself. How I don't feel important to me.

Why have I allowed myself to carry this all with me?

It takes time. I know.

Patience, though

that is a virtue.

Love is sweet.

Love is kind.

Love is patient.

Love is blind.

Love is trusting.

Love is loyal.

If you are reading or listening to this and you think "no, it is not" during those first six lines, then my dear you are experiencing the wrong kind.

Do not doubt love because you have laid in bed with one whom uses it as a mask. Rather, doubt those who have given you a reason to put a question mark on such a strong four-letter word.

If you experience *real* love you will know.

So, doubt the dozen roses because of the hole in the wall you've had to patch up 3 times.

Doubt those Ray-Ban sunglasses because of the bruises you have to excuse as "love bites"

Doubt that new skin-tight dress lying on your bed because of all the other skin-tight dresses that were meant for you but given to someone else behind your back.

Doubt the new ps4 with some new realistic games because of the ps3 that was destroyed because you didn't ask "how was your day, babe?"

See,

Love is not painful.

Love is not spiteful.

Love is not impatient.

Love is not bruises and stitches.

Love is not dismissing.

Love is not taking advantage.

Typically,

Love makes everything ohkay.
It shines, it saves you.
Stop doubting love and start doubting the hate impersonating it.

I need my privacy.

I need my space.

What fucking part of that *don't* you understand?

You hover over me like a lost puppy.

You're so rude.

Haven't you ever heard of bubble space?

Yeah, neither do I *now*...

You popped mine.

I just want to be alone for once,

I can't even take a joke because you crawled up my ass.

I don't *need* you.

I don't *want* you.

You are a fucking loser.

And that is how you make me feel.

You make me feel worthless,

You make me feel disgusting,

As if I am not good enough

Why can't you just leave me be?

It is obvious you cannot read because every time I put the "do not disturb" sign on my door

You barge on in anyways!

If I could put a restraining order on you I would.

Unfortunately, though, that is not possible

Can't you just go?

I need my privacy

...please

Can't you knock?

Can't you warn me?

I never even wanted to meet you.

But you just *had* to meet me.

You introduced yourself to me four years ago.

"hello, my name is depression"

Little did I know that when I shook your hand, I'd be stuck with you.

No matter what I do.

I am sorry to be such a burden.

but, you see, sometimes I cannot think;

not properly anyhow.

Sometimes I cannot decide if I want to dress up or scrub.

Sometimes I do not know what I am actually doing.

A lot of times I don't know if I want to cry,

or hold it all in.

Even a small task such as eating is like a chore.

I hadn't washed my hair in 3 days almost four because tears are all my eyes wanted to pour.

Do I want to wear these socks or those socks?

does it really matter?

No. not really.

oh, but it does, and panic comes in floods; all I need are hugs

or maybe do some drugs

Or maybe I can turn back to my little silver friend with the sharp end

Then maybe I can take this pain away again.

I'm glad some people love me,

Because if they didn't who would?

Not I.

Sad to say, sad to read, even more sad to feel but I have explained before I cannot help this lack of self-love, I have explained before this pain that lies over me like a soaking wet quilt.

I can explain no further, I just have to continue through and through with these weights riding my shoulders.

Maybe someday self-love will find me and maybe not.

I've learned to grow content with that

.

I can love and love and love and still have love to give but when I turn to me, I have none I care to give.

I'm glad some people love me,

Because if they didn't who would?

I am so sad.

It is really hard to cope.

I mean, it is weighing so heavy on me.

Nothing is helping.

I just want to curl up in a ball

I just want to climb mount Everest and fucking scream

I just want to jump off a bridge

I just want to take a razor to my wrist

I am so sad.

I don't know what to do with myself.

From dawn to dusk, my heart will rust.

Overnight, it will heal.

When the sun begins to rise, and I open my eyes

This depression, again, has begun.

I am back at square one.

It just feels like I am

Falling apart.

Day by day

Minute by minute

Quicker by the hour

Like I am a city

Being washed out

by a tsunami

and each wave that rises

Packs a painful punch

A punch that even

the strongest man alive

couldn't take.

And it defeats me

Every.

Single.

Time.

I am slowly forgetting how to even swim

I hope someone offers a life jacket soon.

Until then

I'll just have to float.

I've come to the realization that maybe I do care for myself, somewhere deep down. Truly.

If I didn't, I probably wouldn't bother to drive properly when I'm floating over the shoulder line on the freeway going 85 without noticing I'm pushing 90 because I feel so sleep deprived.

I've told myself, time and time again, I hate myself, never once have I told me I don't care about myself without feeling something burn inside me.

That burning sensation gives me some light, it is telling me to have some patience, to give my brain some time to process this issue that is happening.

This depression just keeps trapping me.

Though, If I look in the mirror and tell myself I love myself that fire turns to dry ice and i think that might just be worse than fire. And it bubbles, and it grumbles, and it causes waves of destruction and I just don't understand this retaliation my body has against those simple words full of warmth and positivity.

Will I ever?

Little darling it will be ohkay.

You do not need to fear

Your emotions

And what they bring to you.

Just smile through the pain and fight against the rain.

Before a hurricane must commence;

Much to my demise

I see you still cannot handle it,

I am losing my voice trying to find you again

I hope you know you are missed

So please, I beg you to come back

I am crying on my knees

Where bruises are forming

And blood is drawing,

Come back so I can be me *again*.

Staring at the mirror only to see my reflection staring back at me

Though my reflection is lacking

As I feel the same these days.

My reflection telling me things I need to hear while my brain is in front of the same mirror whispering lies while sharpening its knives.

And with every clink those knives make

The hairs on my neck begin to rise and with every positive word my refection repeats to me, my brains negativity starts to die

Oh, but when I turn away those words begin to fade and I am drowning in words, words saying things I don't want to hear.

Maybe if I strap this mirror to my face, the negativity will stop, and my reflection can keep telling me kind things because I cannot bare to see my eyes melt to mush, nor the corners of my lips drag across this filthy floor.

Not any longer.

Not anymore.

He says I do not need a filter to look pretty;

He says I am beautiful the way I am.

I tell him I beg to differ.

I continue applying mascara to my already full eyelashes;

'I want to *feel* pretty."

I say.

So, he grabs my hand and takes away my mascara brush,

He picks me up and sits me on the counter top

"you are beautiful *the way you are"*

The words flow from his lips

Like smoke from a raging fire

So soft, so smooth, so harsh with truth.

But are you?

My conscious asked after I screamed at myself telling myself I am a fuck up.

Convincing myself I am a failure.

But am I?

You are not.

I am.

No. I wouldn't say you are.

Then what am I

A friend,

a daughter,

an aunt,

a lover,

a poet,

a caregiver,

an inspiration,

strong,

brave,

powerful,

amazement,

the sun when it sets and the moon when it rises.

You are... human.

Am I?

You are

I am.

Scars are beautiful.

No matter how many there are or how bad they are.

They're beautiful.

Just like your soul, darling.

Don't let anyone dull that shine of yours, the little bit you're holding onto.

Don't let those dirty looks cling onto you, just throw them right back.

And to any girl who needs to hear it:

you are wanted,

you are valid,

you are beautiful,

you matter

And to any boy who needs to hear it:

you too are wanted,

valid,

beautiful,

you too matter.

Scars are beautiful, we should wear them proudly.

Not be ashamed for falling in a hole we didn't see was there.

Your arms are marked with tiger stripes as are your legs and your ribs and breasts.

As are your thighs, and your feet and your torso.

Scars are beautiful, and they visibly prove you're a soldier.

We can't be called soldiers without putting up a fight.

So, keep on marching soldiers, Keep on fighting.

Stop denying your strength, Stop defying the war.

Let it go through, because the longer you hold back the harder it will be.

Scars are beautiful just like you and me.

Maybe.

Maybe I will be ohkay.

I don't know.

I don't know anymore.

I don't know a damn thing.

Maybe,

Maybe someday I will be ohkay.

But who knows?

Not I.

Wow.

How divine, my twisted spine

Bending over backwards wasting my love

on those who never deserved it.

Not even the benefit of the doubt.

I have been so down,

Yet I am fine now.

Just kidding.

I am only pretending.

I suppose I've mastered the art of that.

In fact, I should probably go grab my mask now

So, I don't show pain.

Please

Please refrain from saying anything.

How did I get here ?

Searching for things in places I don't reserve the right to.

Searching for something to take this pain *away*

Something to ease my pain,

Something to sooth my soul

but I'm looking in all the wrong places

and of course, I *know* that, but I have no interest in stopping.

I'm looking for help from things

that aren't meant to help.

"You have to go to a doctor for that."

But-

I don't want a doctor,

no.

I don't want to go.

I don't want to ask for help again

...the same kind that failed before.

I refuse to heal with depression meds

and maybe I shouldn't but I'm more afraid of the side effects

because I'm already so afraid of my illness

... the thoughts that come with it.

I don't want to test myself

and spend the money I don't have on all these pills that are meant to "fix " me.

I am searching for help,

not the kind you'd think,

I'm searching for a way to keep my eyes off the blades,

I'm searching for things to muffle my wretched screams.

I'm beginning to push people away

 Not something I do usually

Don't know why I think it will take away this pain

 I just

want to be alone at all hours of the day

I just

want to ignore my pain and hope it all just fades away

but some days are just too tough to hold on

 To bare this hate I cherish so deeply in my soul

So, I never will know what it feels like in my heart to have a hole.

 I'm made of stone,

 self-love is never shown

It's never learned

 Always burned

Down to ashes,

My emotions spin and swirl and begin to mash in.

And I can't imagine a place to be to take away my insecurities

 So, I scroll on IG and see All these things to make me believe

I'm not perfect but I'm worth it

and I don't have to Make myself match these girls online

Cause on my own I know I can shine

 I can be unique and that's where you find real beauty.

 I wish it was that easy,

To feel like I can be myself and I'll be fine.

 To *choose* happy,

 But that's not how it works.

You have to drown in order to find that first.

And it hurts,

to feel so alone,

To feel so weak.

To feel so worthless.

Not wanting to speak.

And I don't want to push anyone away,

but it's how I'm beginning to deal with this pain

I'm closing up again,

My walls are not coming down.

I want to sit now,

I'm too weak to stand.

I need your help,

Please lend me a hand.

Emotions evoked in sadness

There is no cure to this madness

....*It's madness*

Or so it seems.

I dream weird dreams

And if I don't, I deal with demons

They keep me up with the stars at night.

My heart in fear for the things my brain wants it to hear

I am my biggest bully

No home schooling

Get me away from here.

Grab the wheel and steer.

My palms are sweaty on this leather cover.

Why am I lying under wetter covers?

Sometimes I feel so alone as if There are no others.

I cannot tell you How much hell I put myself through

To wear this smile and lie through my teeth

Just to build up enough energy to respond with

"I'm fine"

I guess I'd rather torture myself Than reach out for *real* help.

How outrageously, insane.

I keep scrambling my brain

Even when it screams

it's in pain.

Intense.

Sorry counselor....

I'm down to 6 cents.

Tell me again,

how am I supposed to pay for this shit?

I am so sorry

That

I am so isolated,

my mind is stated in a dangerous place

                        and

I need some help but when I ask, I fall silent.

I don't know what to do.

Or

what to say.

So, I go and sit in my private little space.

Quite as a mouse,

holding back tears I'm sure could pour for years

... but I won't let them.

And I am starting to block out my feelings, so I don't feel pain anymore.

I won't let myself cry over not being able to see my dad for a year or so at a time,

I won't let myself cry over a goodbye.

                        I won't.

So instead of feeling pain, I choose not to feel at all.

I block the emotions out and pin them to my wall

before they get the chance to flood in at all.

And if I crack, I mustn't stay

I need to go be by myself.

You know

...

Isolate.

Cry, baby

Cry.

Run those eyes

High

And dry

Cry, baby.

You

Crybaby

You.

Do what you need

To do

Cry

And

Cry.

No need to try

Anything new

Just

Fucking

Cry, baby

Cry

To the stars in the

Sky

Wide and divine

You cry so much

Over

Things so little

Why won't you mention

Your emotions get

In the

Middle?

You

 Crybaby

 You

No, it's nothing new.

What is it

That's bothering

You?

Don't hold it in

Like

You often

Convince

Yourself to do.

You

Crybaby

You.

How did I get here ?

Searching for things in places I don't reserve the right to.

Searching for something to take this pain away

something to ease my brain,

something to sooth my soul

but I'm looking in all the wrong places and of course I *know* that but I have no interest in stopping. I'm looking for help from things that aren't meant to help.

You have to go to a doctor for that.

But I don't want a doctor, no I don't want to go. I don't want to ask for help again

the same kind that failed before. I refuse to heal with depression meds and maybe I shouldn't but I'm more afraid of the side effects because I'm already so afraid of my illness,

and the thoughts that come with it.

I don't want to test myself and spend the money I don't have on all these pills that are meant to "fix" me.

I'm searching for help, not the kind you'd think, I'm searching for a way to keep my eyes off the blades, I'm searching for things to muffle my wretched screams.

Dealing with Insanity

spilling profanity on the vanity

I'm so clumsy

I'm so sorry

I didn't mean to snap at you

I'm just trying to get back to her .

but she keeps trying to slip away on hazy days

depression in my brain suffocates me

like a pair of tight skinny jeans on a hot sunny day

I am screaming at her to stop fucking running away

but

lately my days have turned from blue to dark gray

stay, please stay

I can't take more pain

every time she turns away, I feel so drained

and the thoughts she leaves me with are quite insane

I don't want to watch my feet when I walk

I want to hold his hand

I want to point at the birds and the trees with my other

but when she goes away, I don't want to bother.

I just push him away and say

"I'm ohkay"

when I clearly am not

because I cannot

stop these thoughts

Because she refuses to run in place.

Can't stand to see such a long face

and I didn't mean to be that way

I'm sorry, babe

so, let me meditate

maybe more like medicate

I'm supposed to put a smile on this face

And mean it

I'm not supposed to change yours.

I keep running into closed doors.

nothing in store here

I'm so sorry dear

my apologies

I wouldn't say it if I didn't mean it

I didn't mean to cause a scene

but

no one knows behind the scenes of my screen

I am simply tinted 5.

Tonight, the moon will rise

with that, we will take some time

your body flesh with mine

 really

I didn't mean to snap at you

but sometimes or most days my brain doesn't give me enough space

And maybe she doesn't want to clean the vanity

maybe she's tired of the spilt profanity.

maybe I could be nicer to her so she can be nicer to you.

So, please...

He had his chance
And he lost it
You did not lose him
You are stronger
You are strong
You are worth more
You are worth something
And if that is something, he cannot see
That is his loss.
He hurt you
And didn't treat you
Like he was supposed to
Otherwise, why would he lie next to you
Yet
Cry about her?
You aren't her, and he wanted her more
Or, so it seemed
But you are better than her,
I hope that's something you will see
He lost the best thing
For him
That could be.
Cry, let it out
Don't hold back the pain,
But don't dwell on it as well.
You are stronger
You are strong.
You will overcome this
No matter how long
It may take.
Just please,
Don't let yourself break

What am I doing here?
My head is spinning,
I can't see so clear.
So close yet so far out of reach
Or is that just a cliché figure if speech?
I don't know anymore
Head still spinning
Thoughts of blood spilling on the floor
And again, with the closed fucking doors.
How many times do I have to do this?
Continue to go through this?
I am growing tired of feeling so low and lucid,
I am confused.
No one told me a maze could ever be so long.
Usually I am good at these things,
Looking at them from the other side.
Nonetheless I am lost
And you don't get service in a place like this
So dark, so cold
deserted to say the least
Unfortunately, enough a map was not on my list.
Don't worry though
    "I'm fine"

My heart hangs heavy

Though I'm not sure why.

It is filled with love and joy

Which I am beginning to struggle

to express.

I wonder why my head

feels like such an unorganized

mess.

I've been so depressed, it's not

even funny

I'm at the point of staying in

bed

and saying "fuck the money"

I've got nothing to care for

when my mind is in a state like this.

But when you see my long, blue

face

and you ask if I'm ohkay,

I try to muck up the courage to lie

But the look in your eyes even

knows that I'm not fine.

Feeling so deep

So blue.

Drowning in no sleep

Unless I am next to you.

So, from here my dear

What is it I am supposed to do?

Fill my feelings of loneliness with rapid warm tears and bruised fists?

Rid of my anger with horrid screams and broken things?

No, but simply

Ignore the depression with a lighter and some green

Avoid the anxiety with some tunes and you holding me.

The one thing that seems to help me hold onto my sanity

Yet, I still refuse to allow you to witness me in such distress.

Now darling, since I am no longer an emotional mess

Would you caress my bare skin after you help my weak self remove this dress?

Salted.
I am so exhausted, dried out and left for nothing.
My desire to feel higher than the clouds
is beyond something I could never imagine,
Lying out in the dry, cold winter winds
And as I begin to shed some tears, so does the sky
Where the light begins to fade in and suddenly it's all ohkay again
But this time will go by fast
The clouds will roll in
And my world will be dull and grey just like before.
Nothing my already sore body can't handle
Salted.
I'm so exhausted.

Dear diary,

 Why do I hurt so much for no reason at all?

Why do I cry when do not need to?

 Why am I such a burden to my own self?

Putting up walls to protect me from me, just to tear them down

And destroy myself all over again.

At least my soul stays pure and true,

I wish my mind could do the same.

I just wanted to thank my parents, my soulmate and my most supportive friends (you know who you are) for being here for me and with me through everything. It's taken a while to get this poetry collection put together and a lot of these poems were written in the worst of times and has become the best outlet I could find.

I would like to thank y'all for your continued support and cheering me on through this book journey!

I would also like to thank my online supporters; you guys have helped me be more open and confident with my work as for sharing my deep emotions and thoughts I choose not to open up about because sometimes it is just better to write it out than talk it out <3

It is a really scary thing to show the world your dark side, but since creating my poetry page on Instagram @soggy.waffle.poetry it helped me open up to a world of fellow poets and self-loathers! (all love here, no judgement, baby!) It has shown me that I am not the only one who is fighting, and I am not doing it alone! It has also connected me to other souls who need or want to be heard but don't know how to speak up!

We got this though, soldiers!

It has become my goal to show the world what the poetry community on Instagram has shown me:

YOU ARE NOT ALONE!

And always remember to SMILE! 😊

Hakuna matata!

CPSIA information can be obtained
at www.ICGtesting.com
Printed in the USA
FFHW021712050419
51530147-56987FF

9 780368 515651